Scripture Sonnets

Selected Scriptures
Poetically Presented

31 Devotional Readings

Sonja,
May these Scripture
Sonnets be a blessing,
Bob Davidson

Robert V. Davidson

Dedicated to

Barbara Chisholm Davidson

Contents

Introduction

It has been said that a sonnet is
a black square on a white page.[1]
And yet it is a thing of beauty
conveying its concise message
through strict Shakespearean
rhyme and meter. This little book
is dedicated to my mother,
Barbara Chisholm Davidson,
who taught me to love both God
and poetry. I pray this devotional
will accomplish the same for you
as the reader.

Psalm 121

Psalm 121

I lift my eyes and look upon the hills
And ask the source of where my help comes from.
My help comes from the Lord and what he wills,
Creator God of heaven, earth, and sun.
He will not let me stumble or fall down;
He will not slumber as he seeks my keep.
His watch care is his ever great renown
And never yields to slumber nor to sleep.
My rest is in the shade of his right hand;
The sun by day will bring me no alarm.
Against the moon at night he takes his stand
And watches o'er my life to bring no harm.
He watches all that my life has in store
And leads me both for now and evermore.

Colossians 3

Colossians 3

We are a chosen people dearly loved
And clothe ourselves in kind humility,
Bearing each other in life's push and shove,
Forgiving when the hurt is felt in me.
We put on love as virtues have their start:
They unify as woes begin to cease.
And Christ can set up rule within the heart
So members of his body live in peace.
We then are moved by thankfulness to teach
And share the message through our joyful songs,
In gratitude of spirit others reach
Revealing him to whom all praise belongs.
And all we do we do as to the Lord
Whether by deed or spoken through the word.

2 Corinthians 4

~3~

2 Corinthians 4

So though we live as bound in jars of clay,
There is a pow'r within that comes from God.
And when we are hard pressed along the way,
We are not crushed or driven to the sod.
The blessing is we never do lose heart
Though outwardly we ever waste away.
Within our bodies God still does his part
Renewing by his Spirit day by day.
And so these light and momentary woes,
That seem to visit without beck or call,
Achieve for us a glory from the blows
Which in the balance far outweighs them all.
And so we fix our eyes on the unseen,
Eternal glory in its brilliant sheen.

Psalm 100

~4~

Psalm 100

We openly shout joy unto the Lord,
In worship offer what to him belongs.
With gladness we come to the one adored
And sing full throated praise our joyful songs.
We know that in our hearts the Lord is God
And he is maker of us one and all.
We yield, his people, as we onward plod
And follow as his sheep his voice and call.
We enter gates into his courts with praise:
The temple sounds with cries of his great name
And with thanksgiving cheer, our voices raise
To celebrate his love's forever fame.
God's faithfulness to us is never lost;
It runs through generations spite the cost.

James 1

James 1

Consider it pure joy when trials come;
They test our faith and make us persevere.
Then when the testing work is finally done,
Our faith will be complete and made mature.
If anyone lacks wisdom, ask of God
And he will give to all who are without.
But your belief when asking can't be flawed,
Or double-minded, or consumed by doubt.
If you are found in humble circumstance,
Take pride in your position which is high.
The rich will become low by happenstance;
Rewarded you will be when God is nigh.
When you have persevered through trials rife,
By loving God, you gain the Crown of Life.

1 Peter 2

~6~

1 Peter 2

You now have tasted that the Lord is good
So rid yourselves of malice and deceit.
Since you as babies crave milk as your food,
Seek pure-in-spirit kind, for growth complete.
So come to Christ who is the living stone,
Chosen by God, but set aside by man;
And join in building a new house that's known
For sacrifices yielded to God's plan.
A royal priesthood you have now become,
A holy nation whose declaring might
Lift praises up on high unto the one
Who called you out of darkness, into light.
You once were not a people of your own;
Now you are God's people, by mercy shown.

Psalm 19

Psalm 19

The heavens speak the glory of our God;
The skies proclaim the work his hands have done.
By day their speech pours out to give him laud,
By night reveal the knowledge of the One
Who without words can make his being known.
He voices through the skies his mighty worth
And so to all his majesty is shown,
Though silently he speaks to all the earth.
A tent is pitched and given to the sun
That like a bridegroom it may have a place,
Or like a champ its given course to run
A circuit in the heavens daily race.
The rising of the sun delights us all
As warming rays upon each gently fall.

Isaiah 40

~8~

Isaiah 40

When my cause seems to be unknown by God,
Why have I not been heard or seen by him?
Could his supposed care just be a fraud?
But his great love for me is not a whim.
He is Creator of the earth and sky.
His understanding is not known by man.
When we are weary, strength comes from on high;
And pow'r he gives according to his plan.
For even youths grow tired and start to mope;
They stumble as young men and downward fall.
But those who in the Lord will find their hope,
Renew their strength to answer life's hard call.
On eagles' wings they lift and soar above;
In strength they walk or run by God's great love.

Isaiah 53

~9~

Isaiah 53

He grew just like a tender shoot will rise;
And out of the dry ground he pushed up higher.
His lack of beauty caused us to despise;
He had no majesty we should desire.
He therefore was rejected by mankind.
A man of suff'ring who knew much of pain,
Disgraced among his people and maligned.
A low esteem seemed all that he could gain.
And surely he took up our agony
And bore the suffering that was our share.
For our transgressions they pierced him with glee,
And crushed him for iniquities we bear.
But by his punishment our peace is sealed;
And by his bloody wounds, we all are healed.

Psalm 23

Psalm 23

With God my Shepherd I do not have lack.
He beckons me lie down in pastures green.
I am refreshed beside calm waters, slack.
He guides me on right paths by hands unseen.
Though through dark valleys sometimes he may lead,
There is no danger causing me to fear.
His rod and staff along with me proceed
And comfort bring as long as he is near.
A table of good things does he prepare
In sight of those who would be enemy.
Anointing oil is poured upon my hair;
He fills my cup of need abundantly.
My days of life enriched by his great love,
Forever in his house I'll dwell above.

Isaiah 55

Isaiah 55

When you experience a fiery thirst,
Come quench it with fresh water from the stream
And eat the richest fare and be well versed
In what it means to live on God's own team.
So seek the Lord who's ready to be found
And call on him while he is coming near.
Let mercy from the Lord on you abound
And pardon from sin cancel every fear.
For his thoughts rise so high above our own,
The height of his own ways we can't acquire.
Then when God's word from his own mouth has flown,
It will accomplish all he does desire.
By his will you go out to live in joy,
And are led forth in peace as his envoy.

Isaiah 61

Isaiah 61

The Spirit of the Lord is upon me
Because he has anointed me with oil
To set the captives in the prisons free
And to proclaim good news to those who toil.
This is the year God's favor will be shown,
Or vengeance on the ones who should receive.
His comfort will be given all who groan,
And mercy tendered upon those who grieve.
A crown of beauty waits instead of ash;
The oil of joy will broken hearts repair.
A garment of bright praise will shine a flash
Diminishing the spirit of despair.
Then oaks of righteousness they will be made,
In order that God's splendor be displayed.

Psalm 139

~13~

Psalm 139

I praise you God for all you did create,
The wonder of the works your hands have made.
I know full well that in things small or great
Your fearful power is there for all displayed.
My inmost being knit within the womb
Was hid away within my mother's care.
And while it seemed contained in earth's deep tomb,
Your weaving hands my body fashioned there.
My frame was not revealed in that dark place,
Your eyes upon me, though as yet unformed.
In secret there I yielded to your grace,
Was finished and awaited to be born.
The days of life that you ordained for me,
Were written down before one came to be.

Hebrews 10

~14~

Hebrews 10

In confidence we enter Holy Place;
The body of our Lord provides the way.
The curtain rent in two by bloody grace
Opens the House of God where he holds sway.
So let us come anew with sincere hearts
In full assurance that our faith provides,
Our guilty conscience cleansed from the old arts,
Our bodies washed in pure water tides.
So let us hold unswerving to the hope
That we upon his promise do profess,
And spur each other on as we now cope
With doing good so others we might bless.
We will continue meeting by God's plan,
Encouraging each other as we can.

Hebrews 12

~15~

Hebrews 12

A cloud of witness surrounds us on high.
So let us rid ourselves of hin'dring things
And shed the sin that tangles as we ply
The race marked out for us, what'ere it brings.
And so we fix our eyes on Jesus' name,
The pioneer - perfecter of our faith,
Endured the cross and scorned its bitter shame
That we might not grow weary in the race.
No discipline seems pleasant at the time.
As sons and daughters hardship God may bring
Which will our hearts and righteousness refine
And prove us to be children of the King.
Now try to live in peace with everyone.
In holiness rejoice in what he's done.

Psalm 8

~16~

Psalm 8

Considering the heavens you have made,
The moon and stars which you have set in place,
How is it mankind in your mind has stayed
And been cared for by your abundant grace?
A little lower than the angels we,
And yet we're crowned with honor from your hand
And have been given rule by your decree
O'er all created works that you have planned.
So placed beneath our feet are all the herds
Of animals that in the wild there be,
And in the sky all of the flocks of birds,
And all the fish that swim paths in the sea.
O Lord, our Lord, majestic is your name,
Renowned in all the earth to your great fame.

Romans 8

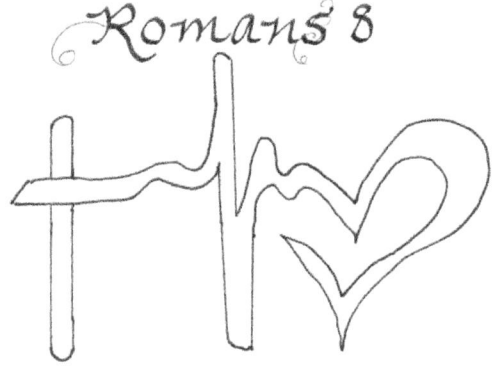

~17~

Romans 8

If God is for us, who can be against?
He did not spare his own son from the stings,
But gave him up for us that in the midst
He will defend against accusing things.
Who then will bring a charge on the elect,
The ones whom God has chosen from the start?
Christ Jesus died, was raised and will perfect
Our verdict through his interceding part.
And who will separate us from God's love?
Will trouble, persecution or the sword?
Our strength to conquer those is from above,
By power given us from Christ our Lord.
So we attached to God shall ever be,
By his great love, for all eternity.

Romans 12

~18~

Romans 12

Considering in view of God's mercy,
To him we owe a living sacrifice.
And so we offer up our own body
For true and proper worship to suffice.
When tempted by world's pattern to conform
We put it to the test to find God's will.
A mind renewed for us he will transform,
His good and perfect pow'r in us fulfill.
If we assess ourselves with highest praise,
We need some sober judgment for that call.
For each have different gifts assigned by grace
Which can be used in serving one and all.
Each member though unique from all the rest,
When unified in body, functions best.

Psalm 103

~19~

Psalm 103

My inmost being lifts praise to the Lord.
His benefits are not forgotten soon—
My sins forgiven and good name restored,
And sickness healed to bring a welcome boon.
He has redeemed my life from hell's deep pit
And crowned me with compassion and his love.
He satisfies desires as he sees fit,
And life renews that we might soar above.
He renders his good deeds so graciously,
Is slow to anger when we go astray.
For sins that cost us so expensively,
He cancels out the debt we cannot pay.
As far then as the East is from the West,
Our sin has been removed, at his behest.

Philippians 4

~20~

Philippians 4

We will rejoice with praise to God and sing.
Let gentleness be evident to all.
We'll not be anxious about anything
But in prayer and petition on him call.
And when we pray, let it be with thanksgiving;
Then God brings peace, in those uncertain times,
Which will transcend our own frail understanding
And in our Lord will guard our hearts and minds.
So finally, we will think on these things:
Whatever is true, noble, and is right,
The pure and the lovely without strings,
Things excellent, praiseworthy in his sight.
And when we practice these thoughts to the end,
The peace of God upon us will descend.

Philippians 4

Philippians 4

Contentment is a practice to be learned
Whatever circumstances we may face,
Whether in need or poverty unearned
Or having plenty in our lives by grace.
The secret to contentment is made known
In every situation life may bring,
Whether we're feeding high upon the bone
Or wanting in our lives for everything.
God is the one who gives us strength through Christ
To find the answers we are searching for.
The riches of his glory come a trice
And meet the needs we have, and those in store.
To God the Father, Son and Holy Ghost
Forever be our praise to the utmost.

Psalm 37

~22~

Psalm 37

Fret not in those who practice evil ways
Or envy others doing what is wrong.
Like grass they wither in the coming days,
Like green plants die away without a song.
Trust in the Lord and do what good you can.
Dwell in the land and bask in pastures sweet.
Delight in God and gifts from his right hand,
Fulfilling your desires and needs to meet.
Commit your ways completely to the Lord
And trust in him and all that he has done.
Then like the dawn will shine your just reward
And vindication like the noonday sun.
Be still and patient waiting for his plan,
Your hope redeemed, inheriting the land.

Ecclesiastes 3

~23~

Ecclesiastes 3

For everything there comes a time to be,
A season set for all that will be done.
And workers toil for small prosperity
And carry burdens God has laid on them.
But everything gains beauty in its time.
Eternity is set in every heart.
And who can fathom what is on God's mind
Or what he's done since time first had its start?
So being happy is a blessed thing
And doing good for others as we live,
For finding joy in eating like a king
And satisfaction in the toil we give.
These are a gift from God's eternal hand,
Unchanging precepts just as he has planned.

Proverbs 3

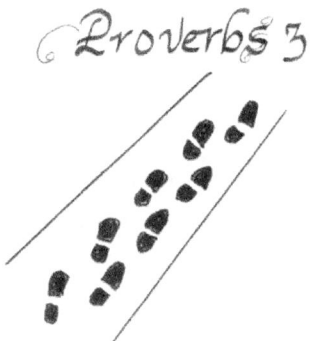

~24~

Proverbs 3

Let wisdom come and ever be your guide,
Prolong your life and bring you years of peace.
Let love and faithfulness in you abide;
Then favor in God's eyes will never cease.
Trust in the Lord applying all your heart.
Lean not on understanding of your own.
Submit to him in acting out your part
And he will make straight paths before you known.
Do not in vain be wise in your own eyes.
Shun evil as you hold the Lord in awe.
Then health of body will become the prize
And nourishment of soul your last hurrah.
The first fruits of your crops to him belong;
Then barns and vats will overflow with song.

Psalm 46

~25~

Psalm 46

Our God is a firm refuge and our strength,
An ever present help when troubles come.
And though the earth be shaken to great length,
We shall not fear though waters roar and foam.
Within a city flows a quiet stream
That's making glad the place the Most High dwells.
God's presence in the city brings esteem,
Defending it when opposition swells.
When nations rage and kingdoms start to fall,
The Lord Almighty is our fortress who
Can make the wars to cease in nations all.
O come and see just what the Lord will do.
Be still and know that God is on the throne,
Exalted among nations—God alone.

Galatians 6

~26~

Galatians 6

When a believer is caught up in sin,
Restore that person with a gentle hand.
But watch yourself that you do not fall in
To similar temptation quite unplanned.
When someone thinks they're something and they're not,
Then they should put their actions to the test
And find their pride in what alone they wrought,
Without comparison to all the rest.
Whatever we have sown, we also reap;
If to the flesh, destruction is to come.
But if the Spirit's pleasure we will seek,
Eternal life with him will be our home.
And so do good to others every day,
Especially fellow travelers of the Way.

Ephesians 2

~27~

Ephesians 2

We once were dead in sin and transgression
And lived and followed in the worldly way.
We gratified the cravings of our passion,
Deserving wrath for going so astray.
But though we were as dead in all our sin,
The great love of our God and his mercy
Made us alive in Christ and raised with him
For seating up on high in realms heav'nly.
By grace, through faith alone, we can be saved;
It is not from ourselves as though the host.
The gift of God from his hand freely gave
That there might be no cause for us to boast.
We are God's handiwork by his design
That we might do good works he will assign.

Psalm 1

~28~

Psalm 1

You must not walk with those who are abhorred,
Nor deem those steeped in sin and mocking right,
But find delight in the law of the Lord
And on it meditate both day and night.
You will be like a tree by water grown
Which yields its fruit each season faithfully.
Your leaf will never wither or fall down
And all you do will thrive abundantly.
The wicked share a mighty different plan:
They are like chaff the wind will blow away.
In judgment they can never take a stand,
Nor with the righteous gather on that day.
The righteous will the watch of God enjoy;
The wicked on their way will he destroy.

John 14

~29~

John 14

When hearts are troubled and we're feeling scared,
We need to place our faith and trust in God.
For many are the rooms he has prepared
For us in glory's mansions, as reward.
Christ went ahead to make a place for us
And in his absence life might seem quite grim.
But he has promised, we believe and thus,
He will come back to take us home with him.
He is alone the truth, the life, the way,
The only access to our Father's place.
And so we seek to worship him each day
While magnifying his almighty grace.
If we know Jesus as God's only son,
We know the Father and the Three in One.

John 15

~30~

John 15

Christ is the vine and we as branches must
Abide in him, the source of all our life.
Then we will have the strength in us to thrust
A fruitful harvest forth amid the strife.
If we in Christ alone do not remain,
We wither on the vine, his power spurned.
Then like dead branches, fruitless and self slain,
We're gathered up, thrown in the fire and burned.
But if we will remain attached to him
And follow his commands without retreat,
Our wishes are fulfilled with holy vim
That he might make our joy in him complete.
No greater love can we have in the end
Than laying down one's life for one's own friend.

Revelation 21

AΩ

~31~

Revelation 21

One day there'll be new heaven and new earth;
The present things will then be passed away.
A Holy City of majestic worth
Will from our God descend on that great day.
God's dwelling place will be among his own
And he himself forever they will gain.
No death nor mourning ever will be known
And there will be no tears and no more pain.
The rule of the old order he'll transcend,
For he is making everything brand new.
He is the one Beginning and the End;
His words are ever trustworthy and true.
Secure then as his children we shall be,
And we shall dwell with him eternally.

Acknowledgements

This undertaking has been a labor of love. There are several people I would like to thank for assisting me along the way:

Barbara Bonebrake for encouraging me to write and for editing the sonnets.

Sara O'Brien for advising and assisting with the self-publishing elements of the book.

Donna Stockin for creating and composing illustrations for the sonnets.

And most of all, my wife, Alice, for helping me forge the first drafts into sonnets that read smoothly, made sense and captured the essence of what the Scriptures had to say.

Notes

[1] *101 Sonnets from Shakespeare to Heaney,* edited by Don Paterson (London: Faber & Faber, 1999), p. xiii.

About the Author

Bob Davidson is a retired general surgeon living with his wife, Alice, in a retirement community in beautiful Upstate New York. They and their children were involved in several short term medical mission trips abroad, especially Haiti. A bout with cancer and chemotherapy has given the author a renewed appreciation for the gift of life. Bob enjoys woodworking, cooking, travel, and poetry. He may be found online at rvdavidson7@gmail.com.

Made in the USA
Middletown, DE
12 March 2019